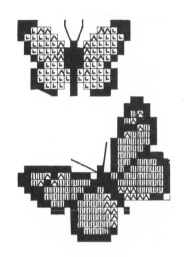

Butterfly Charted Designs

From the Archives of the Lindberg Press

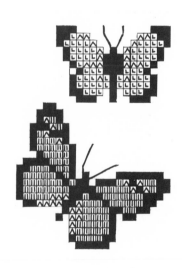

DOVER PUBLICATIONS, INC. • New York

Copyright © 1988 by Dover Publications, Inc.
All rights reserved under Pan American and International Copyright Conventions.

Published in Canada by General Publishing Company, Ltd., 30 Lesmill Road, Don Mills, Toronto, Ontario.
Published in the United Kingdom by Constable and Company, Ltd.

Butterfly Charted Designs is a new work, first published by Dover Publications, Inc., in 1988.

Manufactured in the United States of America
Dover Publications, Inc., 31 East 2nd Street, Mineola, N.Y. 11501

Library of Congress Cataloging-in-Publication Data

Butterfly charted designs.

1. Needlework—Patterns. 2. Butterflies in art. I. Lindberg Press.
TT773.B87   1988   746.44   88-3840
ISBN 0-486-25639-1

Introduction

The butterfly, with its air of fragility and its jewel-like colors, ranks as one of nature's most beautiful creations. The designs in this collection include many well-known favorites like the Monarch butterfly and the Red Admiral butterfly, as well as more exotic species such as the Red Lacewing butterfly and the *Ornithoptera paradisea*, both from New Guinea. In addition to butterflies from around the world, charts are also given for the Tiger and Ctenuchid moths and for the delicate *Palpares imperator*.

The butterflies are shown both singly and combined to form borders, circles, bands and allover patterns, and can be used to create pillows, pictures, bellpulls, placemats and many other decorative accessories.

Most of these designs were originally created for counted cross-stitch, but they are easily translated into other needlework techniques. Keep in mind that the finished piece will not be the same size as the charted design unless you are working on fabric or canvas with the same number of threads per inch as the chart has squares per inch. With knitting and crocheting, the size will vary according to the number of stitches per inch.

COUNTED CROSS-STITCH

MATERIALS

1. **Needles.** A small blunt tapestry needle, No. 24 or No. 26.

2. **Fabric.** Evenweave linen, cotton, wool or synthetic fabrics all work well. The most popular fabrics are aida cloth, linen and hardanger cloth. Cotton aida is most commonly available in 18 threads-per-inch, 14 threads-per-inch and 11 threads-per-inch (14-count is the most popular size). Evenweave linen comes in a variety of threads-per-inch. To work cross-stitch on linen involves a slightly different technique (see page 5). Thirty thread-per-inch linen will result in a stitch about the same size as 14-count aida. Hardanger cloth has 22 threads to the inch and is available in cotton or linen. The amount of fabric needed depends on the size of the cross-stitch design. To determine yardage, divide the number of stitches in the design by the thread-count of the fabric. For example: If a design 112 squares wide by 140 squares deep is worked on a 14-count fabric, divide 112 by 14 (= 8), and 140 by 14 (= 10). The design will measure 8″ × 10″. The same design worked on 22-count fabric measures about 5″ × 6½″.

3. **Threads and Yarns.** Six-strand embroidery floss, crewel wool, Danish Flower Thread, pearl cotton or metallic threads all work well for cross-stitch. DMC Embroidery Floss has been used to color-code the patterns in this volume; a conversion chart for Royal Mouliné Six-Strand Embroidery Floss from Coats & Clark, and Anchor Embroidery Floss from Susan Bates appears on page 48. Crewel wool works well on evenweave wool fabric. Danish Flower Thread is a thicker thread with a matte finish, one strand equaling two of embroidery floss.

4. **Embroidery Hoop.** A wooden or plastic 4″, 5″ or 6″ round or oval hoop with a screw-type tension adjuster works best for cross-stitch.

5. **Scissors.** A pair of sharp embroidery scissors is essential to all embroidery.

PREPARING TO WORK

To prevent raveling, either whip stitch or machine-stitch the outer edges of the fabric.

Locate the exact center of the chart (many of the charts in this book have an arrow at the top or bottom and side; follow these arrows to their intersection to locate the chart center). Establish the center of the fabric by folding it in half first vertically, then horizontally. The center stitch of the chart falls where the creases of the fabric meet. Mark the fabric center with a basting thread.

It is best to begin cross-stitch at the top of the design. To establish the top, count the squares up from the center of the chart, and the corresponding number of holes up from the center of the fabric.

Place the fabric tautly in the embroidery hoop, for tension makes it easier to push the needle through the holes without piercing the fibers. While working continue to retighten the fabric as necessary.

When working with multiple strands (such as embroidery floss) always separate (strand) the thread before beginning to stitch. This one small step allows for better coverage of the fabric. When you need more than one thread in the needle, use separate strands and do not double the thread. (For example: If you need four strands, use four separated strands.) Thread has a nap (just as fabrics do) and can be felt to be smoother in one direction than the other. Always work with the nap (the smooth side) pointing down.

For 14-count aida and 30-count linen, work with two strands of six-strand floss. For more texture, use more thread; for a flatter look, use less thread.

EMBROIDERY

To begin, fasten the thread with a waste knot and hold a short length of thread on the underside of the work, anchoring it with the first few stitches (*Diagram 1*). When the thread end is securely in place, clip the knot.

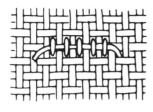

DIAGRAM 1
Reverse side of work

To stitch, push the needle up through a hole in the fabric, cross the thread intersection (or square) on a left-to-right diagonal (*Diagram 2*). Half the stitch is now completed.

Next, cross back, right to left, forming an X (*Diagram 3*).

DIAGRAM 2

DIAGRAM 3

DIAGRAM 4

Work all the same color stitches on one row, then cross back, completing the X's (*Diagram 4*).

Some needleworkers prefer to cross each stitch as they come to it. This method also works, but be sure all of the top stitches are slanted in the same direction. Isolated stitches must be crossed as they are worked. Vertical stitches are crossed as shown in *Diagram 5*.

DIAGRAM 5

At the top, work horizontal rows of a single color, left to right. This method allows you to go from an unoccupied space to an occupied space (working from an empty hole to a filled one), making ruffling of the floss less likely. Holes are used more than once, and all stitches "hold hands" unless a space is indicated on the chart. Hold the work upright throughout (do not turn as with many needlepoint stitches).

When carrying the thread from one area to another, run the needle under a few stitches on the wrong side. Do not carry thread across an open expanse of fabric as it will be visible from the front when the project is completed.

To end a color, weave in and out of the underside of the stitches, making a scallop stitch or two for extra security (*Diagram 6*). When possible, end in the same direction in which you were working, jumping up a row if necessary (*Diagram 7*). This prevents holes caused by stitches being pulled in two directions. Trim the thread ends closely and do not leave any tails or knots as they will show through the fabric when the work is completed.

A number of other counted-thread stitches can be used in cross-stitch. Backstitch (*Diagram 8*) is used for outlines, face details and the like. It is worked from hole to hole, and may be stitched as a vertical, horizontal or diagonal line.

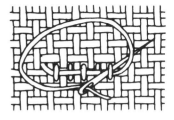

DIAGRAM 6
Reverse side of work

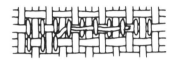

DIAGRAM 7
Reverse side of work

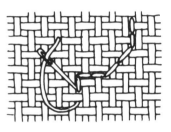

DIAGRAM 8

Straight stitch is worked from side to side over several threads (*Diagram 9*) and affords solid coverage.

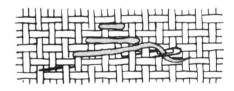

DIAGRAM 9

Lazy daisy stitch and chain stitch (*Diagram 10*) are handy for special effects. Both are worked in the same manner as on regular embroidery.

Lazy Daisy Stitch

Chain Stitch

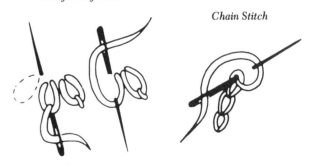

DIAGRAM 10

Embroidery on Linen. Working on linen requires a slightly different technique. While evenweave linen is remarkably regular, there are always a few thick or thin threads. To keep the stitches even, cross-stitch is worked over two threads in each direction (*Diagram 11*).

DIAGRAM 11

As you are working over more threads, linen affords a greater variation in stitches. A half-stitch can slant in either direction and is uncrossed. A three-quarters stitch is shown in *Diagram 12*.

DIAGRAM 12

Diagram 13 shows the backstitch worked on linen.

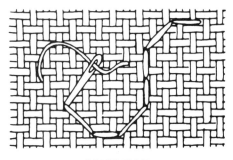

DIAGRAM 13

Embroidery on Gingham. Gingham and other checked fabrics can be used for cross-stitch. Using the fabric as a guide, work the stitches from corner to corner of each check.

Embroidery on Uneven-Weave Fabrics. If you wish to work cross-stitch on an uneven-weave fabric, baste a lightweight Penelope needlepoint canvas to the material. The design can then be stitched by working the cross-stitch over the double mesh of the canvas. When working in this manner, take care not to catch the threads of the canvas in the embroidery. After the cross-stitch is completed, remove the basting threads. With tweezers remove first the vertical threads, one strand at a time, of the needlepoint canvas, then the horizontal threads.

NEEDLEPOINT

One of the most common methods for working needlepoint is from a charted design. By simply viewing each square of a chart as a stitch on the canvas, the patterns quickly and easily translate from one technique to another.

MATERIALS

1. **Needles.** A blunt tapestry needle with a rounded tip and an elongated eye. The needle must clear the hole of the canvas without spreading the threads. For No. 10 canvas, a No. 18 needle works best.

2. **Canvas.** There are two distinct types of needlepoint canvas: single-mesh (mono canvas) and double-mesh (Penelope canvas). Single-mesh canvas, the more common of the two, is easier on the eyes as the spaces are slightly larger. Double-mesh canvas has two horizontal and two vertical threads forming each mesh. The latter is a very stable canvas on which the threads stay securely in place as the work progresses. Canvas is available in many sizes, from 5 mesh-per-inch to 18 mesh-per-inch, and even smaller. The number of mesh-per-inch will, of course, determine the dimensions of the finished needlepoint project. A 60 square × 120 square chart will measure 12″ × 24″ on 5 mesh-to-the-inch canvas, 5″ × 10″ on 12 mesh-to-the-inch canvas. The most common canvas size is 10 to the inch.

3. **Yarns.** Persian, crewel and tapestry yarns all work well on needlepoint canvas.

PREPARING TO WORK

Allow 1″ to 1½″ blank canvas all around. Bind the raw edges of the canvas with masking tape or machine-stitched double-fold bias tape.

There are few hard-and-fast rules on where to begin the design. It is best to complete the main motif, then fill the background as the last step.

For any guidelines you wish to draw on the canvas, take care that your marking medium is waterproof. Nonsoluble inks, acrylic paints thinned with water so as not to clog the mesh, and waterproof felt-tip pens all work well. If unsure, experiment on a scrap of canvas.

When working with multiple strands (such as Persian yarn) always separate (strand) the yarn before beginning to stitch. This one small step allows for better coverage of the canvas. When you need more than one piece of yarn in the needle, use separate strands and do not double the yarn. For example: If you need two strands of 3-ply Persian yarn, use two separated strands. Yarn has a nap (just as fabrics do) and can be felt to be smoother in one direction than the other. Always work with the nap (the smooth side) pointing down.

For 5 mesh-to-the-inch canvas, use six strands of 3-ply yarn; for 10 mesh-to-the-inch canvas, use three strands of 3-ply yarn.

STITCHING

Cut yarn lengths 18″ long. Begin needlepoint by holding about 1″ of loose yarn on the wrong side of the work and working the first several stitches over the loose end to secure it. To end a piece of yarn, run it under several completed stitches on the wrong side of the work.

There are hundreds of needlepoint stitch variations, but tent stitch is universally considered to be *the* needlepoint stitch. The most familiar versions of tent stitch are half-cross stitch, continental stitch and basket-weave stitch.

Half-cross stitch (*Diagram 14*) is worked from left to right. The canvas is then turned around and the return row is again stitched from left to right. Holding the needle vertically, bring it to the front of the canvas through the hole that will

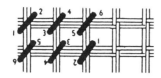

DIAGRAM 14

be the bottom of the first stitch. Keep the stitches loose for minimum distortion and good coverage. Half-cross stitch is best worked on a double-mesh canvas.

Continental stitch (*Diagram 15*) begins in the upper right-hand corner and is worked from right to left. The needle is slanted and always brought out a mesh ahead. The resulting stitch appears as a half-cross stitch on the front and as a slanting stitch on the back. When the row is complete, turn the canvas around to work the return row, continuing to stitch from right to left.

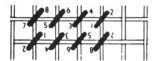

DIAGRAM 15

Basket-weave stitch (*Diagram 16*) begins in the upper right-hand corner with four continental stitches (two stitches worked horizontally across the top and two placed directly below the first stitch). Work diagonal rows, the first slanting up and across the canvas from right to left, and the next down and across from left to right. Moving down the canvas from left to right, the needle is in a vertical position; working in the opposite direction, the needle is horizontal. The rows interlock, creating a basket-weave pattern on the wrong side. If the stitch is not done properly, a faint ridge will show where the pattern was interrupted. On basket-weave stitch, always stop working in the middle of a row, rather than at the end, so that you will know in which direction you were working.

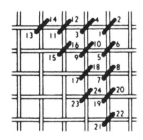

DIAGRAM 16

KNITTING

Charted designs can be worked into stockinette stitch as you are knitting, or they can be embroidered with duplicate stitch when the knitting is complete. For the former, wind the different colors of yarn on bobbins and work in the same manner as in Fair Isle knitting. A few quick Fair Isle tips: (1) Always bring up the new color yarn from under the dropped color to prevent holes. (2) Carry the color not in use loosely across the wrong side of the work, but not more than three or four stitches without twisting the yarns. If a color is not in use for more than seven or eight stitches, it is usually best to drop that color yarn and rejoin a new bobbin when the color is again needed.

CROCHET

There are a number of ways in which charts can be used for crochet. Among them are:

SINGLE CROCHET

Single crochet is often seen worked in multiple colors. When changing colors, always pick up the new color for the last yarn-over of the old color. The color not in use can be carried loosely across the back of the work for a few stitches, or you can work the single crochet over the unused color. The latter method makes for a neater appearance on the wrong side, but sometimes the old color peeks through the stitches. This method can also be applied to half-double crochet and double crochet, but keep in mind that the longer stitches will distort the design.

FILET CROCHET

This technique is nearly always worked from charts and uses only one color thread. The result is a solid-color piece with the design filled in and the background left as an open mesh. Care must be taken in selecting the design, as the longer stitch causes distortion.

AFGHAN CROCHET

The most common method here is cross-stitch worked over the afghan stitch. Complete the afghan crochet project. Then, following the chart for color placement, work cross-stitch over the squares of crochet.

OTHER CHARTED METHODS

Latch hook, Assisi embroidery, beading, cross-stitch on needlepoint canvas (a European favorite) and lace net embroidery are among the other needlework methods worked from charts.

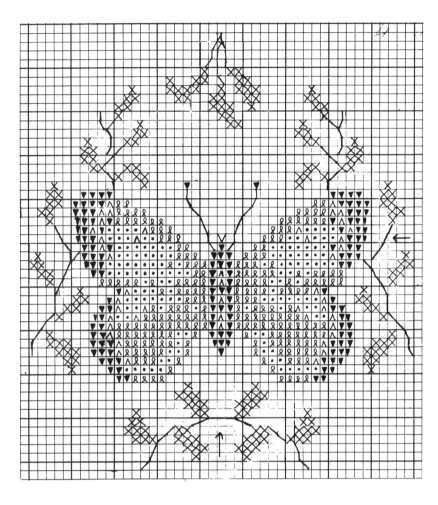

◀ Adonis Blue Butterfly

Back-stitch	Cross-stitch	DMC #	
	▨	334	Medium Marine Blue
	⊡	3325	Baby Blue
	◪	356	Medium Terra-cotta
—	▼	414	Dark Steel Gray
—	⊠	989	Light Forest Green

Work back-stitches in antennae with 414 Dark Steel Gray; work back-stitches in branches with 989 Light Forest Green.

Butterfly Repeat Pattern ▶

Back-stitch	Cross-stitch	DMC #	
\ or /	◭	581	Moss Green
	⊡	742	Light Tangerine
	⊟	900	Dark Burnt Orange
	■	938	Ultra Dark Coffee Brown
—	◉	801	Dark Coffee Brown
	⊞	435	Very Light Brown

Work back-stitches in antennae with 801 Dark Coffee Brown; work back-stitches in background in 581 Moss Green.

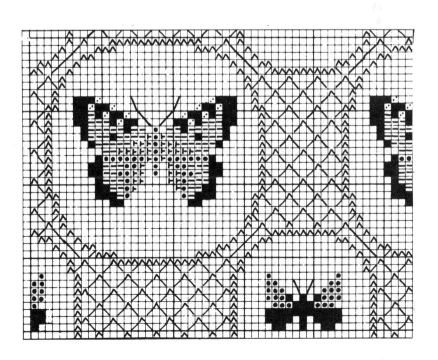

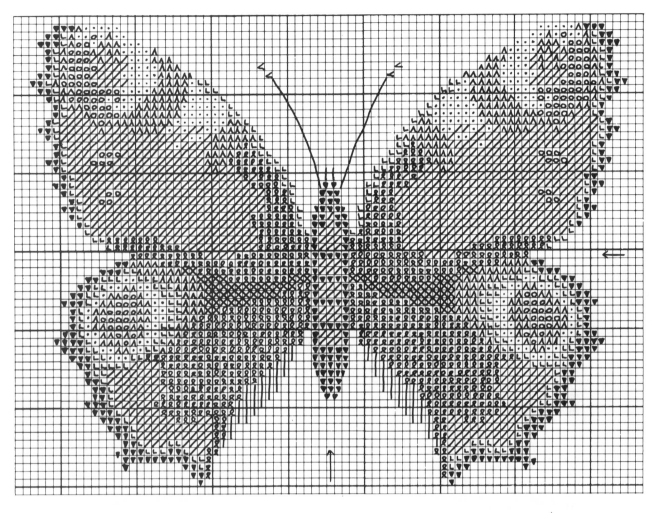

◀ Butterfly Placemat

Back-stitch	Cross-stitch	DMC #	
	⊡	407	Medium Cocoa Brown
– – –	◣	610	Very Dark Drab Brown
——	◰	3032	Medium Mocha Brown
	⌊	422	Light Hazelnut Brown
	Ⓢ	725	Topaz
	⊡	937	Medium Avocado Green
	△	470	Medium Light Avocado Green
	⊓	471	Light Avocado Green
	⊠	906	Medium Parrot Green
	⊞	581	Moss Green
	·	3024	Very Light Brown Gray
	⫼	3687	Mauve
	⊠	3688	Medium Light Mauve

▲ Peacock Butterfly

Back-stitch	Cross-stitch	DMC #	
	·	444	Dark Lemon Yellow
——	▼	801	Dark Coffee Brown
	◰	433	Medium Brown
	⊠	434	Light Brown
	⊓	436	Tan
	⊡	813	Light Blue
	△	3051	Dark Gray Green
	⌊	3053	Gray Green

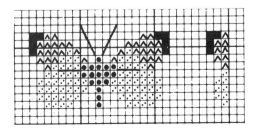

◀ Butterfly Border

Back-stitch	Cross-stitch	DMC #	
——	·	646	Dark Beaver Gray
	△	740	Tangerine
	■	780	Very Dark Topaz
	··		White

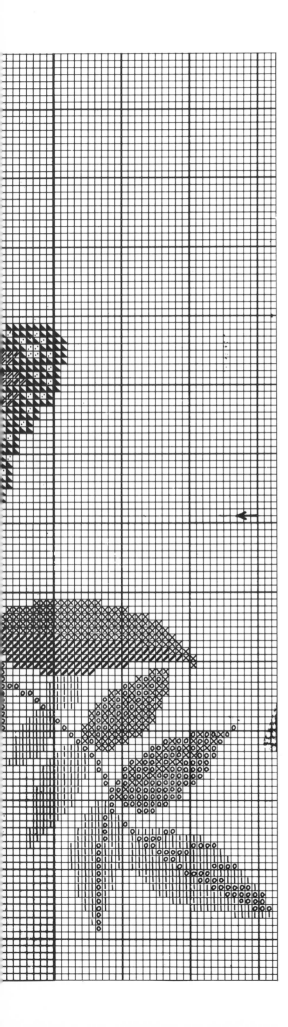

◄ Monarch Butterfly

Back-stitch	Cross-stitch	DMC #	
	◪	310	Black
	⊠	581	Moss Green
	⊠	471	Light Avocado Green
	Ⅱ	472	Very Light Avocado Green
——	K	733	Medium Olive Green
	⊙	734	Light Olive Green
	⊡	938	Ultra Dark Coffee Brown
	⊘	920	Medium Copper
	⊞	921	Copper
	⊿	922	Light Copper
	⊠	977	Light Golden Brown
	Ⓢ	3687	Mauve
	⊟	3326	Light Rose
	⊠	963	Very Light Dusty Rose
	⊡		Ecru

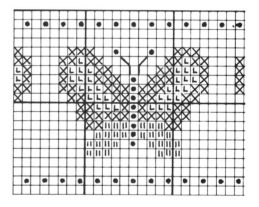

▲ Butterfly Edging

Back-stitch	Cross-stitch	DMC #	
	⊠	741	Medium Tangerine
	Ⓛ	972	Yellow Orange
——	⊡	921	Copper
	Ⅲ	977	Light Golden Brown

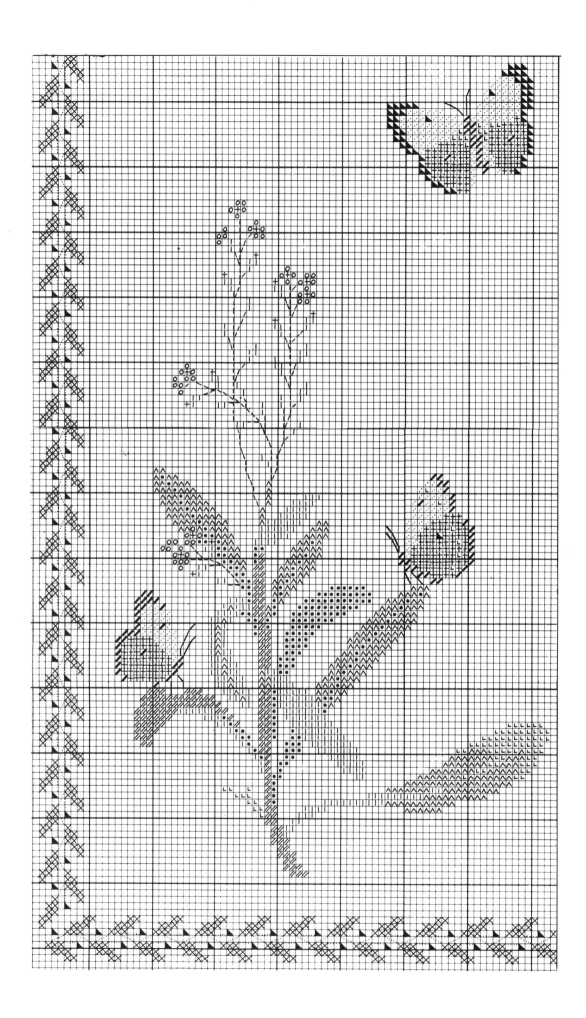

◀ Placemat with Sulphur Butterflies

Back-stitch	Cross-stitch	DMC #	
	⊡	554	Light Violet
	◣	938	Ultra Dark Coffee Brown
——	◪	433	Medium Brown
·······	⊑	832	Dark Golden Wheat
	⊞	725	Topaz
	⊡	726	Light Topaz
	⊠	906	Medium Parrot Green
	◨	3346	Hunter Green
– – –	△	470	Medium Light Avocado Green
	⊔	471	Light Avocado Green
	◺	581	Moss Green

▲ Old World Swallowtail Butterfly

Back-stitch	Cross-stitch	DMC #	
	⊡	335	Rose
	ⱴ	676	Light Old Gold
	⊙	826	Medium Blue
——	⊠	844	Ultra Dark Beaver Gray
——	⊡	644	Medium Beige Gray
	◪	{ 646	Dark Beaver Gray
		647	Medium Beaver Gray
			Use 1 strand of each color
	◺	{ 676	Light Old Gold
		648	Light Beaver Gray
			Use 1 strand of each color

Work back-stitches in antennae with 644 Medium Beige
Gray; work back-stitches in wings with 844 Ultra Dark
Beaver Gray.

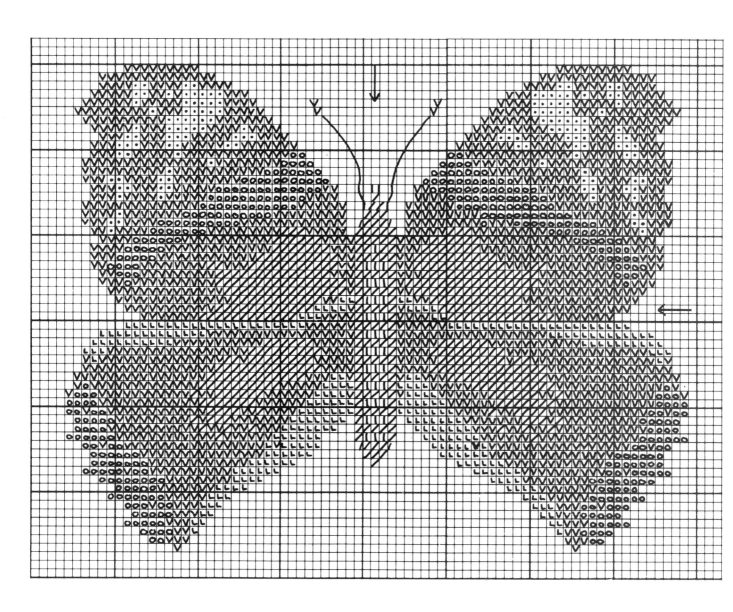

▲ Red Admiral Butterfly

Back-stitch	Cross-stitch	DMC #	
	⊻	938	Ultra Dark Coffee Brown
——	⊿	801	Dark Coffee Brown
	⊓	433	Medium Brown
⌞	{ 433	Medium Brown
	435	Very Light Brown
			Use 1 strand of each color
	◎	900	Dark Burnt Orange
	⊡		Ecru

Mourning Cloak Butterflies and Roses ▶

Back-stitch	Cross-stitch	DMC #	
	■	310	Black
	⊓	347	Dark Salmon
	⊠	3328	Medium Salmon
	⊟	351	Coral
	⊿	352	Light Coral
	⊠	353	Peach
	⊡	677	Very Light Old Gold
——	◉	898	Very Dark Coffee Brown
〜〜	⊞	611	Dark Drab Brown
	◤	3345	Dark Hunter Green
	◪	987	Medium Forest Green
	⊠	988	Forest Green
	⊡	3347	Medium Yellow Green
	◎	581	Moss Green
	⊠	927	Medium Gray Blue

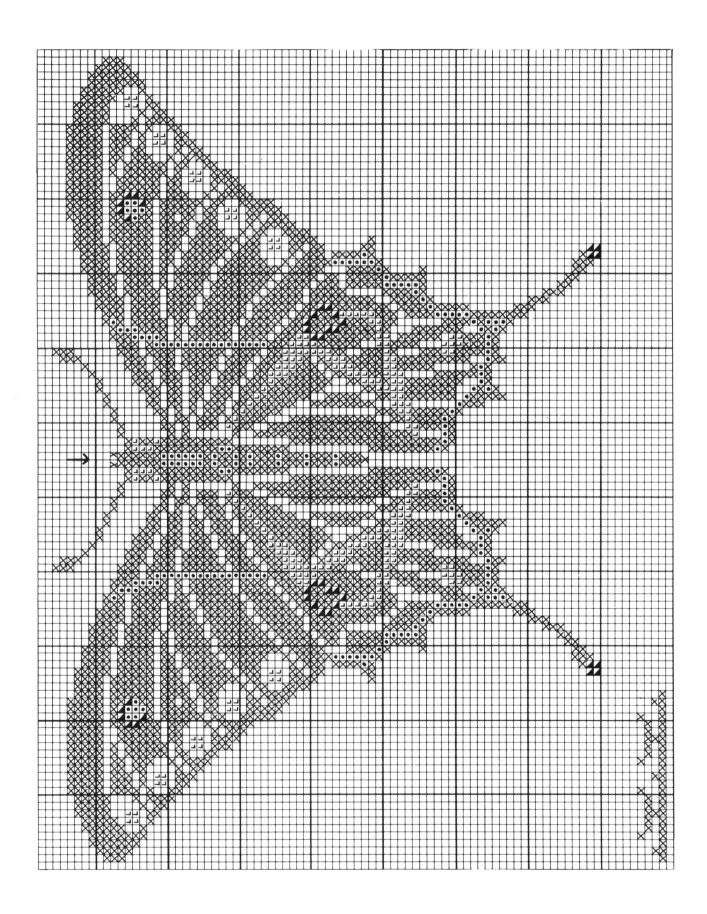

Cross-stitch		DMC #	
◨		606	Bright Orange Red
◉		797	Royal Blue
⊠		938	Ultra Dark Coffee Brown
⊡		973	Bright Canary Yellow

▼ **Butterfly Notebook Cover**

Back-stitch	Cross-stitch	DMC #	
	▣	640	Very Dark Beige Gray
	▨	642	Dark Beige Gray
	⊠	644	Medium Beige Gray
	⊠	{ 642	Dark Beige Gray
——		644	Medium Beige Gray
			Use 1 strand of each color
	▧	744	Medium Yellow
	◉	813	Light Blue
	▨	3348	Light Yellow Green
	▨	{ 3347	Medium Yellow Green
		3348	Light Yellow Green
			Use 1 strand of each color
	▨		White

Note: This design is best worked on linen (see page 5), since some of the stitches are moved over one thread.

Butterfly Border ◀

Back-stitch	Cross-stitch	DMC #	
	◉	309	Deep Rose
	⊡	602	Medium Cranberry
	⊠	915	Dark Plum
——			

17

Butterfly Wreath

Back-stitch	Cross-stitch	DMC #	
++++	■	310	Black
	⊠	208	Very Dark Lavender
	⊡	209	Dark Lavender
•-•-•	◣	610	Very Dark Drab Brown
	⊞	611	Dark Drab Brown
	⊙	797	Royal Blue
	△	798	Dark Delft Blue
	⊟	799	Medium Delft Blue

Back-stitch	Cross-stitch	DMC #	
	⊡	891	Dark Carnation Pink
---	⊠	927	Medium Blue Gray
	⊠	972	Yellow Orange
——	⊞	3012	Medium Khaki Green
	⊠	3024	Very Light Brown Gray
	⊡		Ecru

Outline wings of butterflies at top in back-stitch with 611 Dark Drab Brown.

Sulphur Butterfly ▶

Back-stitch	Cross-stitch	DMC #	
——	■	435	Very Light Brown
	◪	742	Light Tangerine
	⊠	444	Dark Lemon Yellow
	⊞	726	Light Topaz
	⊡	905	Dark Parrot Green
	L	906	Medium Parrot Green
	⊡	907	Light Parrot Green

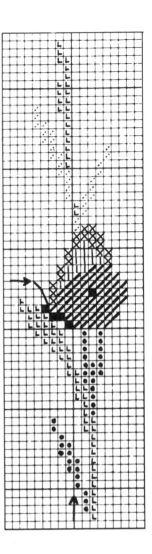

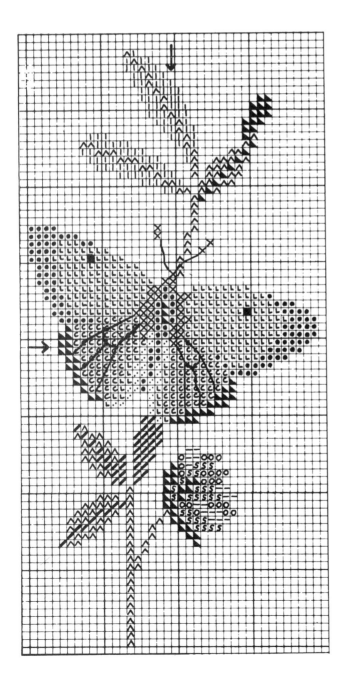

◀ Sulphur Butterfly and Rosebud

Back-stitch	Cross-stitch	DMC #	
	S	309	Deep Rose
	○	335	Rose
	–	894	Very Light Carnation Pink
	c	742	Light Tangerine
	L	444	Dark Lemon Yellow
	⊡	677	Very Light Old Gold
	◣	611	Dark Drab Brown
	⊡	612	Medium Drab Brown
——	⊠	680	Dark Old Gold
	■	828	Very Pale Blue
	◪	3346	Hunter Green
	◮	906	Medium Parrot Green
	⊞	907	Light Parrot Green

Bellpull with Monarch and Little Sulphur Butterflies

Back-stitch	Cross-stitch	DMC #	
	L	444	Dark Lemon Yellow
———	■	938	Ultra Dark Coffee Brown
	Ⅲ	921	Copper
	△	977	Light Golden Brown
	◪	986	Dark Forest Green
	⊠	3346	Hunter Green
	⊙	3347	Medium Yellow Green
	◣	3011	Dark Khaki Green
	⊡	734	Light Olive Green
	⊟	581	Moss Green
	⊡	3326	Light Rose
	⊠	776	Medium Pink

Butterflies and Flowers

Back-stitch	Cross-stitch	DMC #	
	⑤	{ 208	Very Dark Lavender
		209	Dark Lavender
			Use 1 strand of each color
	Ⅴ	350	Medium Coral
++++	▼	801	Dark Coffee Brown
	◖	975	Dark Golden Brown
	◎	976	Medium Golden Brown
	⊡	977	Light Golden Brown

Back-stitch	Cross-stitch	DMC #	
——	⊠	433	Medium Brown
✦✦✦	⊞	434	Light Brown
	⊠	988	Forest Green
	◁	989	Light Forest Green
	⊿	{ 988	Forest Green
		989	Light Forest Green
			Use 1 strand of each color

21

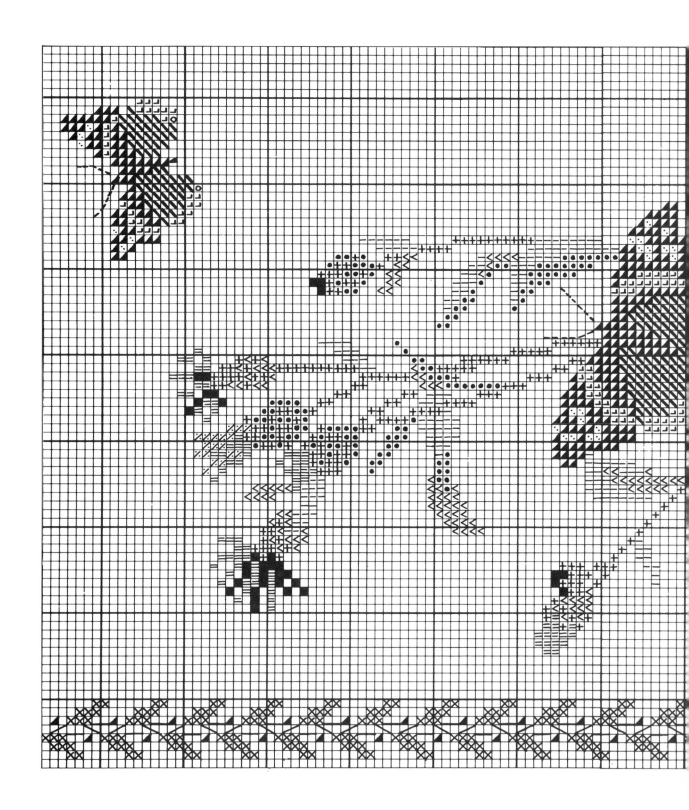

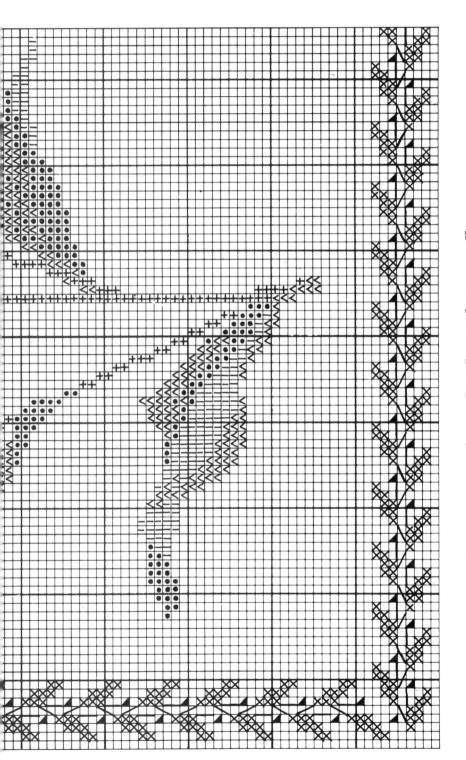

Placemat with Red Admiral Butterflies

Back-stitch	Cross-stitch	DMC #	
	☒	316	Medium Antique Mauve
	■	552	Dark Violet
	Ⅲ	208	Very Dark Lavender
	●	580	Dark Moss Green
	☒	581	Moss Green
	⊓	471	Light Avocado Green
	☒	906	Medium Parrot Green

Back-stitch	Cross-stitch	DMC #	
	⊞	3012	Medium Khaki Green
	⊙	798	Dark Delft Blue
	⊔	900	Dark Burnt Orange
	◣	938	Ultra Dark Coffee Brown
	◩	801	Dark Coffee Brown
‒ ‒ ‒	⦂		White

Checkered Skipper

Back-stitch	Cross-stitch	DMC #		Back-stitch	Cross-stitch	DMC #	
	◤	208	Very Dark Lavender		⊠	3046	Medium Yellow Beige
	‖	210	Medium Lavender		⊘	3347	Medium Yellow Green
	⊓	211	Light Lavender		⊟	3348	Light Yellow Green
——	◣	839	Dark Beige Brown	——	⊠	{ 3347	Medium Yellow Green
——	⊘	841	Light Beige Brown			3348	Light Yellow Green
	◹	842	Very Light Beige Brown				Use 1 strand of each color

Work back-stitches on wings with 839 Dark Beige Brown, back-stitches in antennae with 841 Light Beige Brown and back-stitches in border with 1 strand each of 3347 Medium Yellow Green and 3348 Light Yellow Green.

Adonis Blue Butterfly

Back-stitch	Cross-stitch	DMC #	
	⊞	415	Pearl Gray
	Y	470	Medium Light Avocado Green
	◪	471	Light Avocado Green
	⊟	472	Very Light Avocado Green
	◪	792	Dark Cornflower Blue
	H	793	Medium Cornflower Blue
	◹	794	Light Cornflower Blue

Back-stitch	Cross-stitch	DMC #	
——	◩	{ 414	Dark Steel Gray
		793	Medium Cornflower Blue
			Use 1 strand of each color
	◉	{ 414	Dark Steel Gray
		840	Medium Beige Brown
			Use 1 strand of each color
——	⊠	{ 3347	Medium Yellow Green
		3348	Light Yellow Green
			Use 1 strand of each color

Work back-stitches in antennae with 1 strand each of 414 Dark Steel Gray and 793 Medium Cornflower Blue; work back-stitches in border with 1 strand each of 3347 Medium Yellow Green and 3348 Light Yellow Green.

Note: This design is best worked on linen (see page 5), since some of the stitches are moved over one thread.

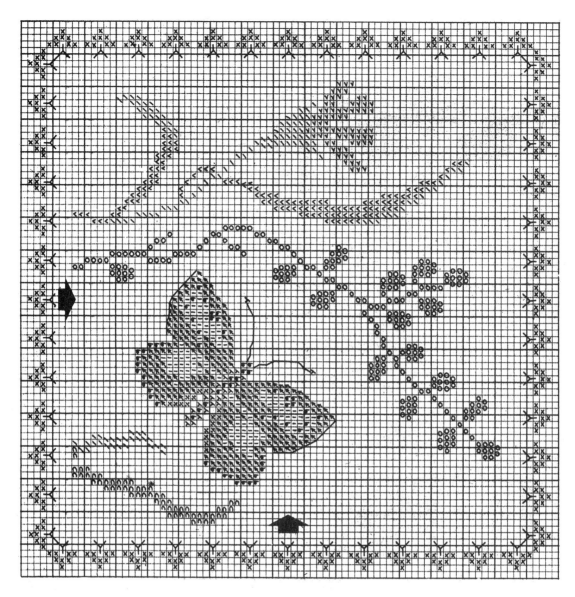

Purple Emperor Butterfly

Back-stitch	Cross-stitch	DMC #	
——	▣	839	Dark Beige Brown
——	⊠	842	Very Light Beige Brown
	⊵	962	Medium Dusty Rose
	⫿	977	Light Golden Brown
	⧠	3347	Medium Yellow Green
	⊙	989	Light Forest Green
	⊿	3348	Light Yellow Green
	◪	{ 351	Coral
		976	Medium Golden Brown
			Use 1 strand of each color

Back-stitch	Cross-stitch	DMC #	
	⊿	{ 977	Light Golden Brown
		3348	Light Yellow Green
			Use 1 strand of each color
	⊏	{ 989	Light Forest Green
		3348	Light Yellow Green
			Use 1 strand of each color
——	⊠	{ 3347	Medium Yellow Green
		3348	Light Yellow Green
			Use 1 strand of each color

Work back-stitches on wings with 839 Dark Beige Brown, back-stitches in antennae with 842 Very Light Beige Brown and back-stitches in border with 1 strand each of 3347 Medium Yellow Green and 3348 Light Yellow Green.

Note: This design is best worked on linen (see page 5), since some of the stitches are moved over one thread.

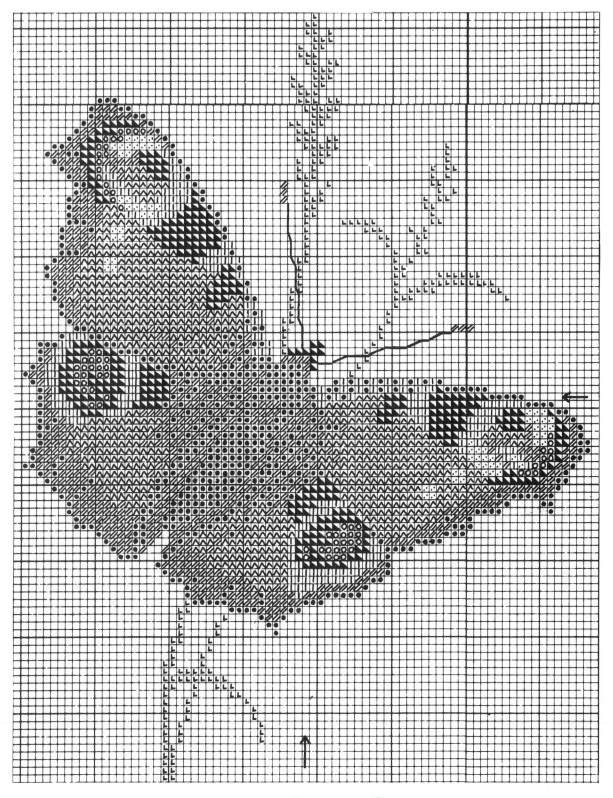

Peacock Butterfly

Back-stitch	Cross-stitch	LMC #		Back-stitch	Cross-stitch	DMC #	
	⊡	793	Medium Cornflower Blue	———	⊠	435	Very Light Brown
	◿	921	Copper		⊞	676	Light Old Gold
	◣	938	Ultra Dark Coffee Brown		⊡	3053	Gray Green
	⊙	801	Dark Coffee Brown		⊡		White

Cabbage Butterflies

Back-stitch	Cross-stitch	DMC #	
	◣	500	Very Dark Blue Green
	◿	986	Dark Forest Green
	⊠	3346	Hunter Green
	⊙	3347	Medium Yellow Green
− − −	⊟	581	Moss Green
	Ⓢ	725	Topaz
	Ⓛ	928	Light Gray Blue
	■	938	Ultra Dark Coffee Brown
	⊡	3326	Light Rose
	◹	776	Medium Pink
	⊓	818	Baby Pink
	⊡		White

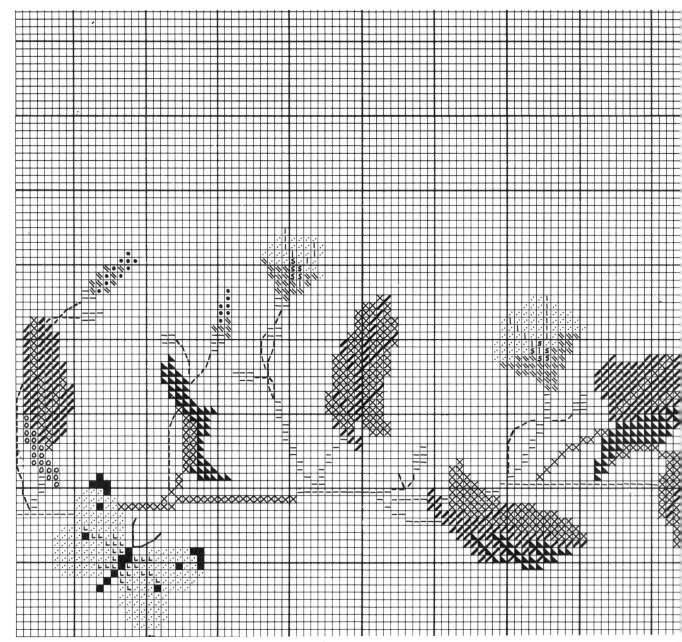

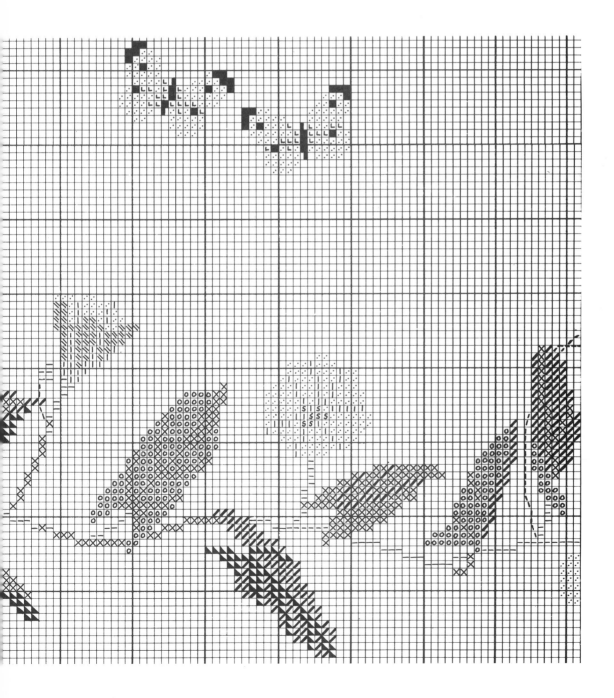

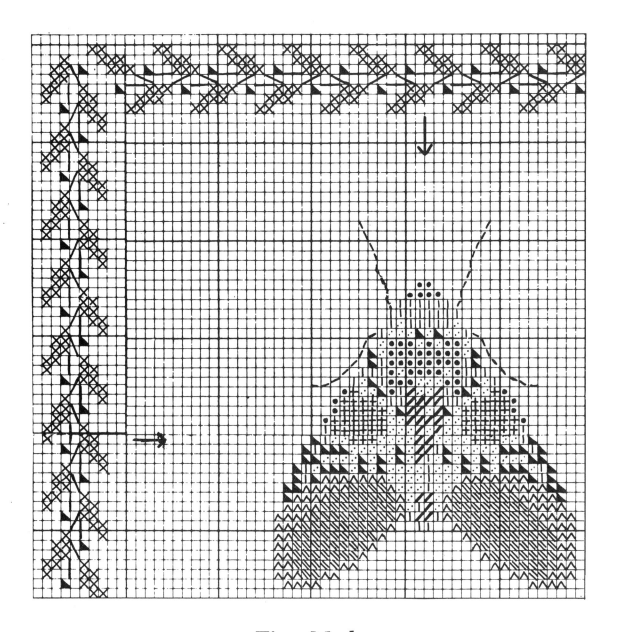

Tiger Moth

Back-stitch	Cross-stitch	DMC #	
	◪	349	Dark Coral
	◩	407	Medium Cocoa Brown
	◭	758	Light Terra-cotta
——	⊡	781	Dark Topaz
	⊞	783	Christmas Gold
	◣	844	Ultra Dark Beaver Gray
– – –	⊡	648	Light Beaver Gray
	⊠	906	Medium Parrot Green
	⊡		White

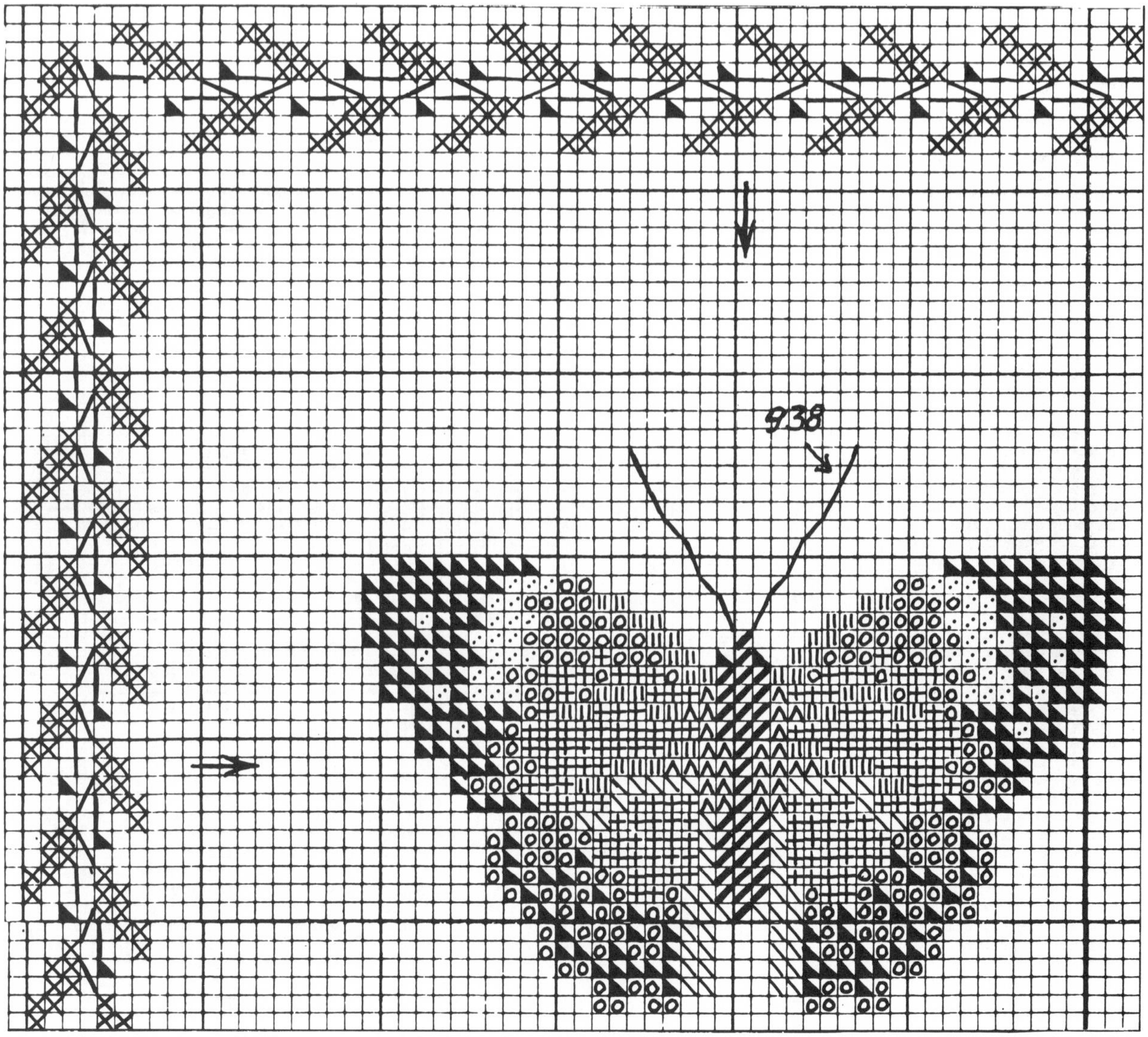

Red Lacewing Butterfly

Back-stitch	*Cross-stitch*	*DMC #*	
	⊞	335	Rose
	▥	350	Medium Coral
	⧅	352	Light Coral
	⊡	792	Dark Cornflower Blue
	⊠	906	Medium Parrot Green
	◪	938	Ultra Dark Coffee Brown
———	⧄	433	Medium Brown
	⍓	435	Very Light Brown
	⊹		White

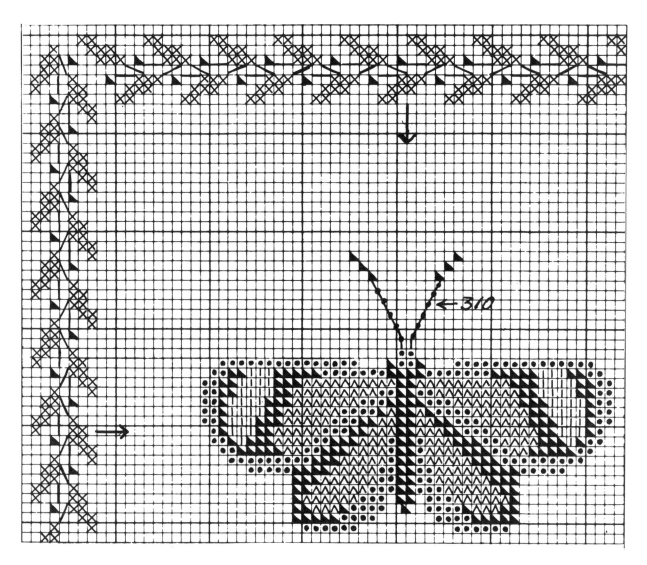

Cartea vitula

Back-stitch	Cross-stitch	DMC #	
┼┼┼┼	◣	310	Black
───	☐	434	Light Brown
	⊡	500	Very Dark Blue Green
	⊠	906	Medium Parrot Green
	⊞	726	Light Topaz
	◿	741	Medium Tangerine

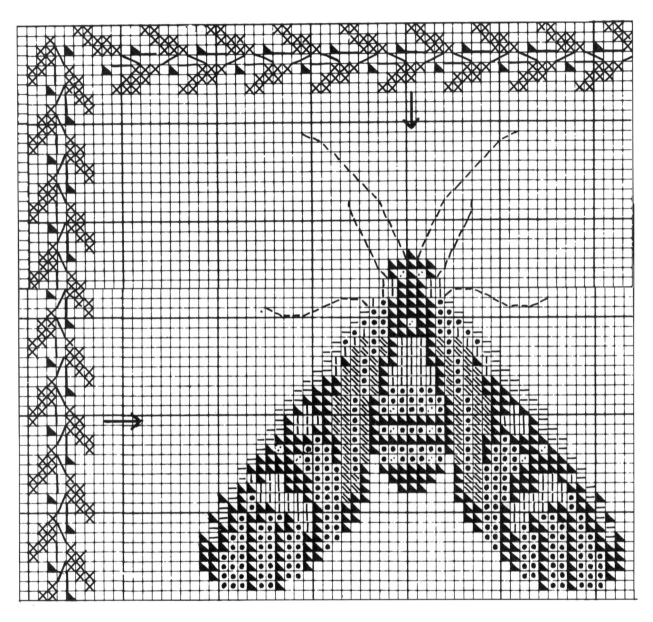

Ctenuchid Moth

Back-stitch	Cross-stitch	DMC #	
	◣	310	Black
	◩	350	Medium Coral
	⊞	676	Light Old Gold
———		780	Very Dark Topaz
	⊡	826	Medium Blue
– – –	⊙	844	Ultra Dark Beaver Gray
	⊠	906	Medium Parrot Green
	⊟	921	Copper

Ornithoptera paradisea

Back-stitch	Cross-stitch	DMC #	
•••••	◣	310	Black
	◪	783	Christmas Gold
	⊡	725	Topaz
	⊠	906	Medium Parrot Green
	◮	907	Light Parrot Green
———	⊙	830	Medium Greenish Brown

Giant Swallowtail Butterfly

Back-stitch	Cross-stitch	DMC #	
	⟁	349	Dark Coral
	🗆	444	Dark Lemon Yellow
	⊡	792	Dark Cornflower Blue
··········	◣	898	Very Dark Coffee Brown
————		780	Very Dark Topaz
	⊠	906	Medium Parrot Green

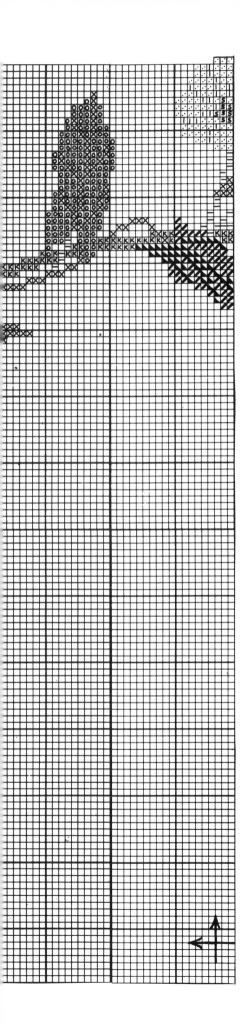

Centerpiece with Cabbage Butterflies

Back-stitch	Cross-stitch	DMC #	
	◣	500	Very Dark Blue Green
	◪	986	Dark Forest Green
	☒	3346	Hunter Green
	◙	3347	Medium Yellow Green
....	⊟	581	Moss Green
	⑨	725	Topaz
	⊡	928	Light Gray Blue
———	■	938	Ultra Dark Coffee Brown
	◙	3326	Light Rose
	◨	776	Medium Pink
	⊞	818	Baby Pink
	Ⓚ	3045	Dark Yellow Beige
	⊡		White

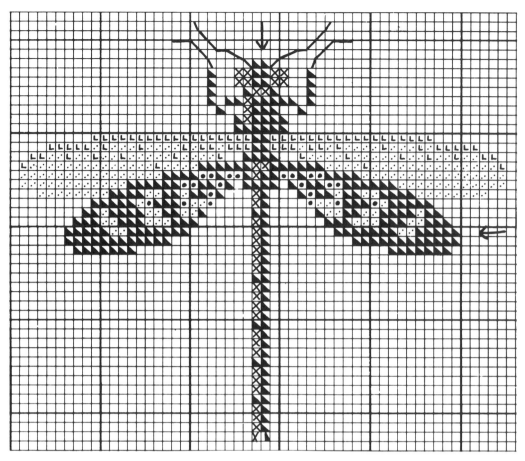

Palpares imperator

Back-stitch	Cross-stitch	DMC #	
	⊡	307	Lemon Yellow
	⊠	355	Dark Terra-cotta
	⊡	518	Light Wedgwood Blue

Back-stitch	Cross-stitch	DMC #	
——	◣	898	Very Dark Coffee Brown
	⌐	612	Medium Drab Brown

Tortoiseshell Butterfly ▶

Back-stitch	Cross-stitch	DMC #	
	▼	3328	Medium Salmon
	⊡	760	Salmon
——	⊠	938	Ultra Dark Coffee Brown

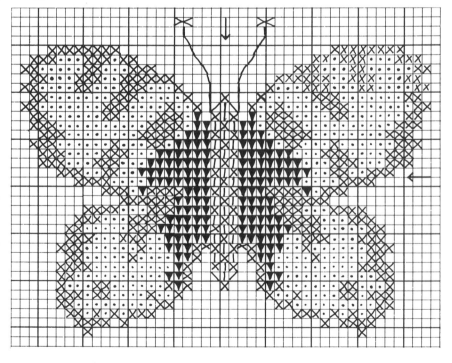

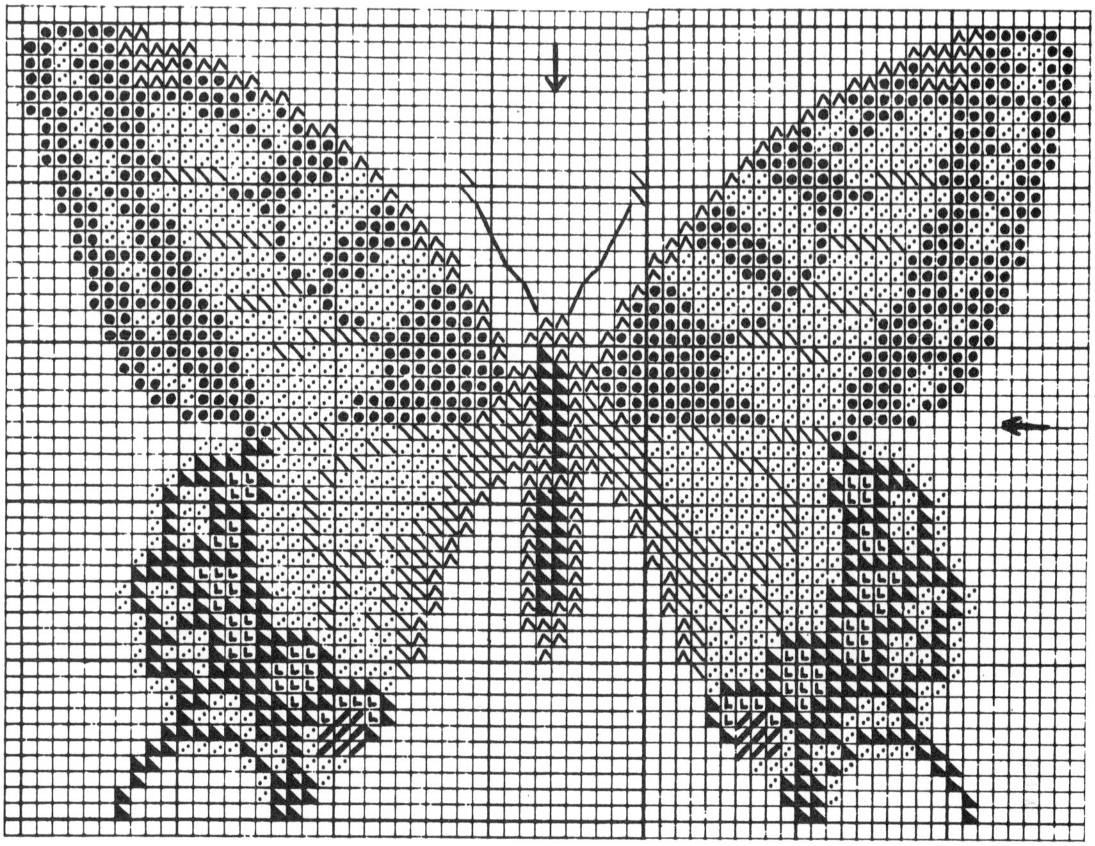

▲ Swallowtail Butterfly

Back-stitch	*Cross-stitch*	*DMC #*	
		304	Medium Christmas Red
——		610	Very Dark Drab Brown
		726	Light Topaz
		734	Light Olive Green
		798	Dark Delft Blue
		844	Ultra Dark Beaver Gray
		898	Very Dark Coffee Brown

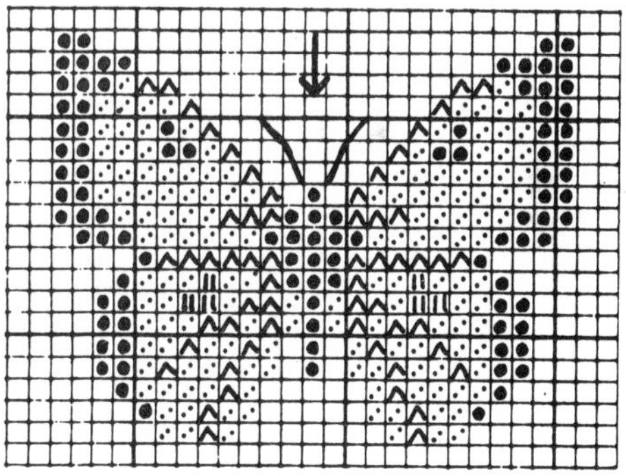

▲ Alfalfa Butterfly

Back-stitch	*Cross-stitch*	*DMC #*	
		307	Lemon Yellow
		734	Light Olive Green
		741	Tangerine
——		898	Very Dark Coffee Brown

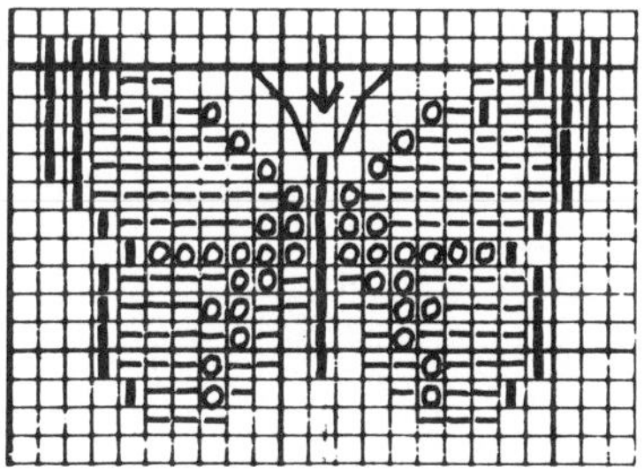

▲ Little Sulphur Butterfly

Back-stitch	*Cross-stitch*	*DMC #*	
		783	Christmas Gold
		742	Light Tangerine
——		801	Dark Coffee Brown

Fantasy Butterflies

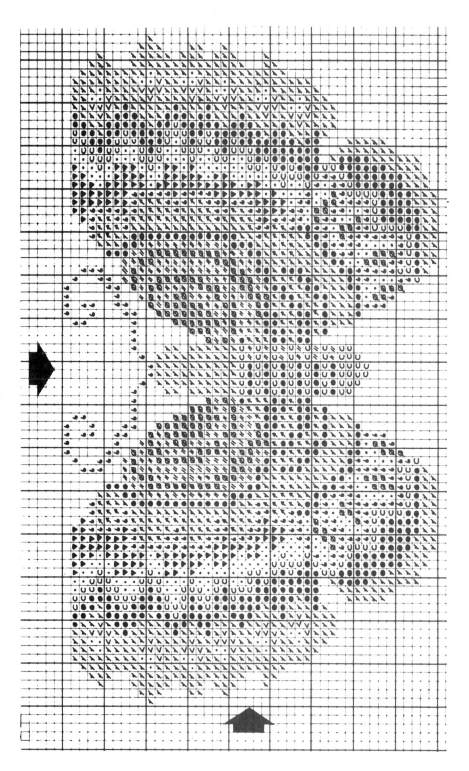

Red Butterfly

Cross-stitch	DMC #	
✈	309	Deep Rose
·	554	Light Violet
▶	718	Plum
◿	602	Medium Cranberry
◙	603	Cranberry

Cross-stitch	DMC #	
◖	703	Chartreuse
c	725	Topaz
●	732	Olive Green
◿	734	Light Olive Green
✈	807	Peacock Blue

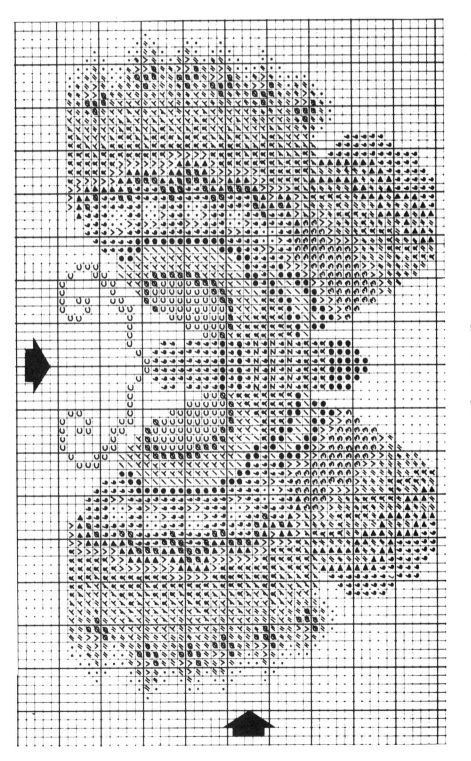

Blue Butterfly

	Cross-stitch	DMC #	
▲		309	Deep Rose
⬛		335	Rose
⬚		351	Coral
●		917	Medium Plum
✕		553	Medium Violet
Z		554	Light Violet
⬗		602	Medium Cranberry

	Cross-stitch	DMC #	
▽		603	Cranberry
⟋		604	Light Cranberry
C		894	Very Light Carnation Pink
◖		703	Chartreuse
⟍		734	Light Olive Green
·		726	Light Topaz
⟋		807	Peacock Blue

41

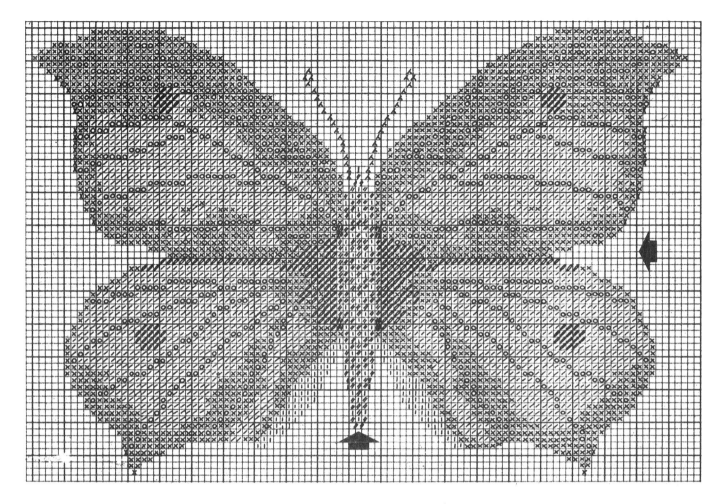

Brimstone Butterfly

Cross-stitch	DMC #		Cross-stitch	DMC #	
◩	350	Medium Coral	▥	644	Medium Beige Gray
▨	680	Dark Old Gold	◪	642	Dark Beige Gray
⊠	729	Medium Old Gold		644	Medium Beige Gray
◹	676	Light Old Gold			Use 1 strand of each color
◩	642	Dark Beige Gray	◙	3072	Very Light Beaver Gray

Note: This design is best worked on linen (see page 5), since some of the stitches are moved over one thread.

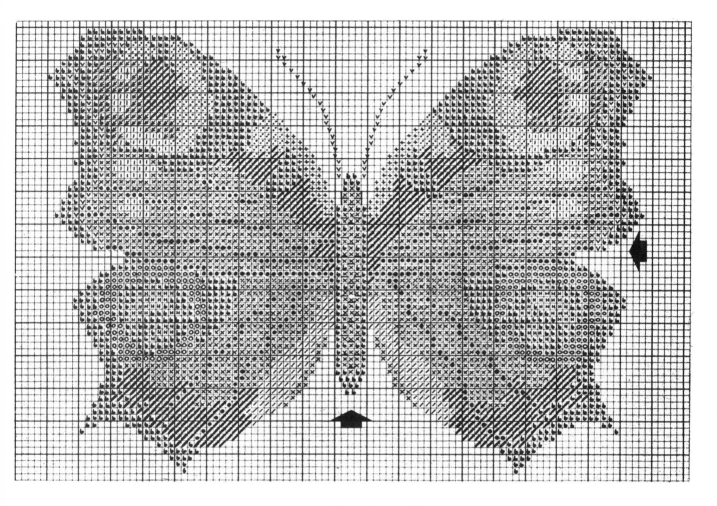

Peacock Butterfly

Note: This design is best worked on linen (see page 5), since some of the stitches are moved over one thread.

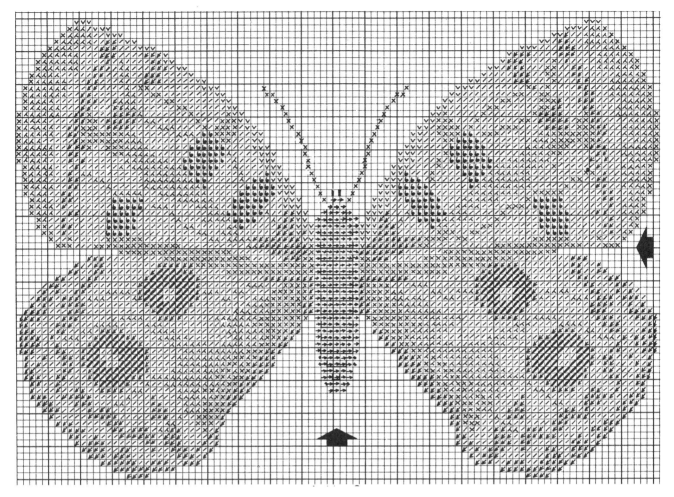

Apollo Butterfly

Back-stitch	Cross-stitch	DMC #	
	◪	350	Medium Coral
	◤	451	Dark Shell Gray
	⊠	452	Medium Shell Gray
	◪	453	Light Shell Gray
	Ⅴ	{ 451	Dark Shell Gray
		453	Light Shell Gray
			Use 1 strand of each color
——	➡	{ 453	Light Shell Gray
		640	Very Dark Beige Gray
			Use 1 strand of each color
	ℭ	{ 451	Dark Shell Gray
		844	Ultra Dark Beaver Gray
			Use 1 strand of each color
	☑		Ecru

Note: This design is best worked on linen (see page 5), since some stitches are moved over one thread.

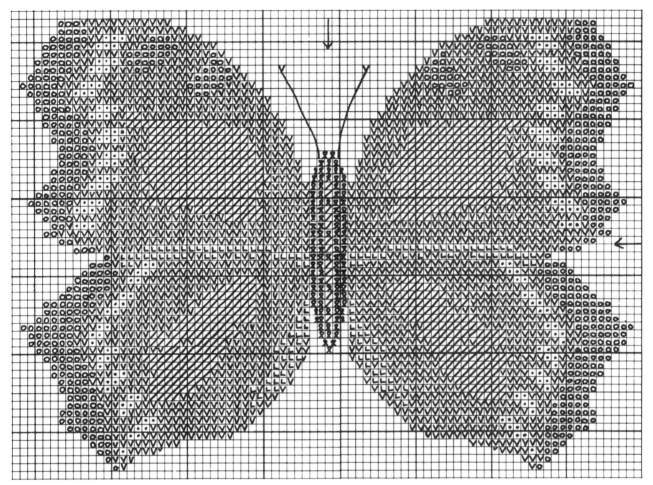

Mourning Cloak Butterfly

Back-stitch	Cross-stitch	DMC #		Back-stitch	Cross-stitch	DMC #	
	⊙	{ 444	Dark Lemon Yellow		⊠	838	Very Dark Beige Brown
		307	Lemon Yellow		⊻	839	Dark Beige Brown
			Use 1 strand of each color	——	⊘	840	Medium Beige Brown
	⊡	817	Very Dark Coral		⌊	841	Light Beige Brown

Note: This design is best worked on linen (see page 5), since some of the stitches are moved over one thread.

Butterfly Matchbox Cover

Back-stitch	Cross-stitch	DMC #		Back-stitch	Cross-stitch	DMC #	
	◩	839	Dark Beige Brown		◲	920	Medium Copper
	◱	644	Medium Beige Gray		⊡	921	Copper
		{ 839	Dark Beige Brown		⊠	922	Light Copper
——	◲	644	Medium Beige Gray		◩	977	Light Golden Brown
			Use 1 strand of each color				

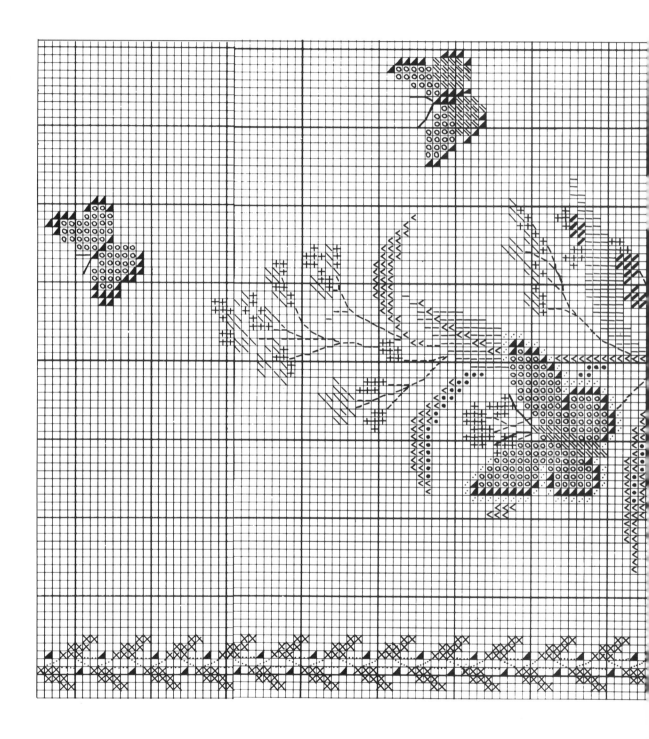

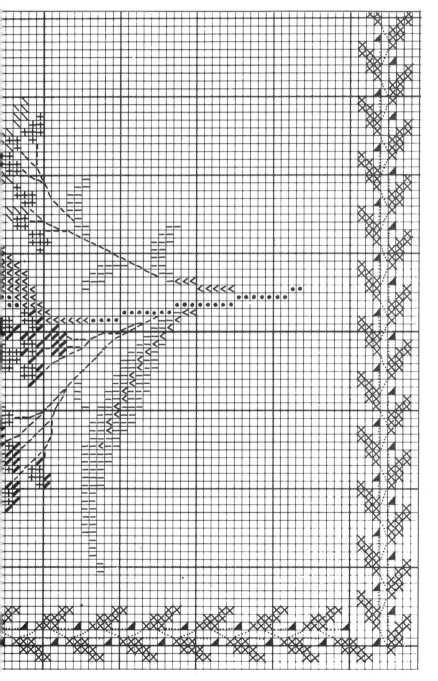

Placemat with Blue Butterflies

Back-stitch	Cross-stitch	DMC #	
	◪	725	Topaz
	⊞	444	Dark Lemon Yellow
	◩	307	Lemon Yellow
	⊡	793	Medium Cornflower Blue
	◤	831	Light Greenish Brown
■		844	Ultra Dark Beaver Gray

Back-stitch	Cross-stitch	DMC #	
	◨	414	Dark Steel Gray
	⊡	415	Pearl Gray
	⊠	906	Medium Parrot Green
	⊡	3346	Hunter Green
	◤	470	Medium Light Avocado Green
	⊞	471	Light Avocado Green

SIX STRAND EMBROIDERY COTTON (FLOSS) CONVERSION CHART

KEY: T = Possible Substitute   * = Close Match   — = No Match

DMC NO.	ROYAL MOULINÉ NO.	BATES/ANCHOR NO.
White	1001	2
Ecru	8600	926
208	3335*	110*
209	3415*	105
210	3320*	104
211	3410	108*
221	2570	897*
223	2555	894
224	2545	893
225	2540	892
300	8330	352*
301	8315*	349*
304	2415*	47*
307	6005*	289*
309	2525*	42*
310	1002	403
311	4275T	149*
312	–	147*
315	3130	896*
316	3120	895*
317	1030*	400*
318	1020*	399*
319	5025	246*
320	4270*	216*
321	2415	47
322	–	978*
326	2530*	59*
327	3365*	101*
333	–	119
334	4250T	145
335	2525T	42*
336	4270*	149*
340	–	118
341	–	117
347	2425*	13*
349	2400	13
350	2045T	11
351	2015T	11*
352	2015	10*
353	2010*	8*
355	8095	351
356	8090	5975*
367	5020	216*
368	5005*	240*
369	5005	213*
370	–	889*
371	–	888*
372	–	887*
400	8325*	351
402	8305*	347*
407	8005	882*
413	1025*	401
414	1020*	400*
415	1015	398
420	8720*	375*
422	8710*	373*
433	8265	371*
434	8210	309
435	8210*	369*
436	8205	363*

DMC NO.	ROYAL MOULINÉ NO.	BATES/ANCHOR NO.
437	8200*	362
444	6155*	291
445	6000	288
451	–	399*
452	–	399*
453	1015T	397*
469	5255	267*
470	5255*	267
471	5245	266*
472	5240	264*
498	2425T	20*
500	5125	879*
501	5120*	878
502	5110	876
503	5105	875
504	5100	213*
517	–	169*
518	4860*	168*
519	4855T	167*
520	–	862*
522	–	859*
523	–	859*
524	1115T	858*
535	–	401*
543	8500	933*
550	3380*	102*
552	3370*	101
553	3360	98
554	3355*	96*
561	–	212*
562	–	210*
563	–	208*
564	–	203*
580	5935	267*
581	5925	266*
597	4860*	168*
598	4855*	167*
600	2225*	59*
601	2225*	78*
602	2640*	77*
603	2720*	76*
604	2710	75*
605	2155	50*
606	7260	335
608	7255	333*
610	5825T	889*
611	5735T	898
612	8815*	832
613	5605*	956*
632	8530	936*
640	8625	903
642	8620*	392
644	8800	830
645	1115	905*
646	1115*	8581
647	1110	8581*
648	1100*	900
666	2405	46
676	6250	891
677	–	886*

DMC NO.	ROYAL MOULINÉ NO.	BATES/ANCHOR NO.
680	6260*	901
699	5375	923*
700	5365*	229
701	5365*	227
702	5330	239
703	5320	238
704	5310*	256*
712	8600*	387*
718	3015*	88
720	–	326
721	–	324*
722	–	323*
725	6215	306*
726	6150*	295
727	6135	293
729	6255	890
730	–	924*
731	–	281*
732	5925T	281*
733	–	280*
734	–	279*
738	8245*	942
739	8240*	885*
740	7045	316
741	6125	304
742	6120	303
743	6210	297
744	6110*	301*
745	6105	300*
746	6100	386*
747	4850	158*
754	8075	778*
758	8080	868
760	2035	9*
761	2030	8*
762	1010*	397
772	–	264*
775	4600*	128*
776	2110*	24*
778	3110	968*
780	8215*	310*
781	8215	309*
782	6230	308
783	6220*	307
791	4165*	941*
792	4155T	940
793	4155	121
794	4145	120*
796	4340	133*
797	4265*	132*
798	4325	131*
799	4250*	130*
800	4310	128
801	8405	357*
806	4870T	169*
807	4860*	168*
809	4145*	130*
813	4610*	160*
814	2340T	44*
815	2530*	43

DMC NO.	ROYAL MOULINÉ NO.	BATES/ANCHOR NO.
816	2530	44*
817	2415T	19
818	2505*	48
819	2000	892*
820	4345	134
822	8605*	387*
823	4400*	150
824	4225	164*
825	4215	162*
826	4210	161*
827	4605	159*
828	4850	158*
829	5825	906
830	5825*	889*
831	5825T	889*
832	5815	907
833	5815*	874*
834	5810*	874
838	8425*	380
839	8560	380*
840	8555	379*
841	8550	378*
842	8505	376*
844	1115T	401*
869	8720*	944*
890	5025*	879*
891	2135	35*
892	2130	28
893	2125*	27
894	2115T	26
895	5430*	246*
898	8425*	360
899	2515	27*
900	7230*	333
902	–	72*
904	5295*	258*
905	5295	258*
906	5285*	256*
907	5280*	255
909	5370	229*
910	5370*	228*
911	5465*	205*
912	5465	205
913	5460*	209
915	3030	89*
917	3020*	89*
918	8330*	341*
919	8095*	341*
920	8060*	339*
921	8060T	349*
922	8315T	324*
924	4830T	851*
926	4820*	779*
927	4810T	849*
928	1010T	900*
930	4510	922*
931	4505	921*
932	4500	920*
934	5070T	862*
935	5225T	862*

DMC NO.	ROYAL MOULINÉ NO.	BATES/ANCHOR NO.
936	5260T	269
937	5260	268
938	8430	381
939	4405	127
943	4935*	188*
945	8020*	347*
946	7230*	332*
947	7255*	330*
948	8070	778*
950	8020T	4146
951	8020T	366*
954	5455*	203*
955	5450	206*
956	2170*	40*
957	2160T	40*
958	–	187
959	–	186
961	2515*	76*
962	2515	76*
963	2505	49*
964	5150*	185
966	5430	214*
970	7040	316*
971	7045	316*
972	6120*	298
973	6015	290
975	8365	355*
976	8355	308*
977	8350	307*
986	5430	246*
987	5020T	244*
988	5295T	243*
989	5405T	242*
991	5165T	189*
992	4925*	187*
993	4915*	186*
995	4710	410
996	4700	433
3011	5525T	845*
3012	5525*	844*
3013	5515	842*
3021	–	382*
3022	–	8581*
3023	–	8581*
3024	1100	900*
3031	–	905*
3032	8620T	903*
3033	8610*	388*
3041	3215*	871
3042	3205*	869
3045	6260T	373*
3046	5810	887*
3047	5805	886*
3051	5530T	846*
3052	5060*	859*
3053	5055*	859*
3064	8005*	914*
3072	4805*	397*
3078	6130	292*
3325	4200	159*

DMC NO.	ROYAL MOULINÉ NO.	BATES/ANCHOR NO.
3326	2115*	25*
3328	2045	11*
3340	–	329
3341	–	328
3345	5025T	268*
3346	5220T	257*
3347	5210*	266*
3348	5270*	265
3350	2220	42*
3354	2210	74*
3362	–	862*
3363	–	861*
3364	8435	843*
3371	–	382
3607	–	87*
3608	–	86
3609	2335	85
3685	2335	70*
3687	2325	69*
3688	2320	66*
3689	2310	49
3705	–	35*
3706	–	28*
3708	–	26*
48	9000*	1201*
51	9014	1220
52	9006	1208
53	–	
57	9002	1203
61	9013T	1218*
62	9000T	1201*
67	–	1211*
69	–	1218*
75	9002	1206*
90	9012T	1217*
91	9008*	1211
92	9011T	1216*
93	9007*	1210*
94	9011*	1216
95	9006T	1208*
99	9005T	1207*
101	9009*	1213*
102	–	1208*
103	–	1210*
104	9012	1217
105	9013*	1218*
106	9002T	1203*
107	9003	1204
108	9014*	1220*
111	9007*	1218*
112	9003T	1204*
113	9007*	1210*
114	9010	1215
115	9004	1206
121	9007	1210
122	9010T	1215*
123	9007T	1213*
124	9009	1210
125	9009	1213
126	9006*	1208*